The House Inside My Head

poems by

Chris Arvidson

Finishing Line Press
Georgetown, Kentucky

The House Inside My Head

Copyright © 2022 by Chris Arvidson
ISBN 978-1-64662-840-7 First Edition
All rights reserved under International and Pan-American Copyright Conventions.
No part of this book may be reproduced in any manner whatsoever without written permission from the publisher, except in the case of brief quotations embodied in critical articles and reviews.

ACKNOWLEDGMENTS

The good people of the Charlotte Mecklenburg Library's Write Like You Mean It and Poetry in Pajamas writing groups, and the Pen to Paper sessions at Charlotte Lit, inspired the poems in this book. Thanks to Pam and Rob at the library, and Kathie & Paul at Charlotte Lit, who so ably lead. Without you guys, the words would have banged around in my head, forever unwritten and unspoken.

An earlier version of the poem "A Definition of Unity" appeared in the anthology *Voices on Unity*, published by Mountain State Press.
"Little Birds" appeared in an *ekphrastic* exhibit at the Mooresville Art Center.
"New Woods Old" appeared in an *ekphrastic* exhibit at the Ashe County Arts Center.

Publisher: Leah Huete de Maines
Editor: Christen Kincaid
Cover Art: Chris Arvidson
Author Photo: Anna Gallant Carter
Cover Design: Elizabeth Maines McCleavy

Order online: www.finishinglinepress.com
also available on amazon.com

Author inquiries and mail orders:
Finishing Line Press
PO Box 1626
Georgetown, Kentucky 40324
USA

Table of Contents

Lake Boat 1

New Woods Old 2

Dear Lake Michigan: 3

Super Blue Pictures 4

The Stucco-Covered Concrete Walls Were Pock-Marked
  and Uneven 5

Jerusalem Dawn 6

My Security 7

I Wish I Could Go On a Walk with Anne Lamott 8

Damp Hands 9

On I-77 10

Stepping Sideways 11

Heart Attack—A Duplex 12

Who We're Going To Be 13

Sunday Morning 14

Holidays 15

On The Way Home from the Doctor's Office 16

A Definition of Unity 18

Little Birds 20

Sunday Night Is Yellow 21

Elmwood Cemetery #1 22

Elmwood Cemetery #2—A Pandemic Sonnet 23

The House Inside My Head 24

Without my Henry, none of this happens.

Lake Boat

Out on the slate surface of Lake Michigan
There on the flat edge of horizon
A smudge of dark pewter moves
Ever so slowly.

How big it must be, the Lake Boat,
That I can see it a mile or more from this beach.
Long and low the dusky angles sit
Marking the blurry place where colorless sky meets grey water.

Big things seem small now
And small ones loom large.
Billions of droplets make up the lake
Hundreds of feet of steel created that boat.

Trillions of grains of sand
Comprise this one short swath of beach
Where my feet make shallow impressions just like those
Of the raccoons and otters who scamper along the edges.

Just little me sits here, my body crusted with grit,
Gazing out at the Lake Boat for so long
That I can discern its movement
Across the plane of smooth water.

New Woods Old

I come from the new woods deep in shadows
Where lost is real
And consequences full near and present.

I come from the new woods
Where paths are few and faint
And those marked are mere suggestions.

I go to the old woods
Where for many thousands of years
Feet and wagons have made paths so clear that to walk them you must climb in.

I go where the old trees have been gone for millennia
Lost to the axe, transformed into tools, ships, fuel, and buildings
Covered over with new kinds of paths.

In their place, a checkerboard beauty of human making
Greens and golds and purples of unimagined variety
Dotted with white puffed animals with dark feet.

In the old woods you are never really lost.
All is before you and the woods remaining are uniform,
Purposeful, cultivated, and minded.

I come from the new woods deep in shadows
Where lost is real
And the consequences full near and present.

Dear Lake Michigan:

Last night I had a hard time falling asleep
I found myself standing on your dark shores
Illuminated by a bright full moon
That cast sparkly bits across your slow little waves
In the slight breeze that blew in to your shore.

Then a surprising thing happened—I rose up and up
Not a being with wings like an angel or bird
Just lighter than air I soared up and over your waters
Holding my hands above my head reaching for the moon
From on high I looked down on your peaceful waters
And saw the life within all around.

I sank back down a bit and saw otters at a creek mouth
They smiled and waved at me floating above them
Further I sank and let the tips of my toes feel your cool water
I flew along your surface and lake trout leaped up alongside me
Laughing as they chased.

Just because I could I soared up again
To a height where I could still hear you, smell you
And lay back in the comforting air
Closed my eyes
And sank slowly, finally,
To sleep.

Super Blue Pictures

The car thermometer read two degrees
The door crackled open and I exited
In a puff of visible breath
The interior instantly dropping to match

The frozen tundra atmosphere heaving to enter
Wanting to capture the full moon at dawn
Over the frozen crust of snow on sand
I trudged into the plethora of darkest blues

In the sky and out on the open water
And the closer undulating waves frozen
Firm in the moment unmoving
Removing one arctic-level glove

To click the shutter I panned the Lake Michigan shoreline
Unusually silent in the icy atmosphere
Where the wind moved water too far away to be heard
In only a few short moments the cold penetrated

For the first time in a life lived
In snow and ice and wind
Feeling a shiver of fear in its grip
Back in the car safely starting to warm

The shiver morphed into tears
Dribbling down still-frosty cheeks
My hand, my hand, blue as the snow on the sand
The pain courting real frostbite.

The Stucco-Covered Concrete Walls Were Pock-Marked And Uneven

Years have passed since their last coat of paint
High, at least 20 feet in the air
On top jagged gruesome
Shards of glass imbedded.

The pointed pieces clear or brown or green
Like the teeth of a dragon or science fiction alien
How would anyone scale a wall this high anyway
And why would they want to?

Inside, a hospital for the dying
A chapel for the nuns and patients
A modest concrete block house
The home of a saint.

Jerusalem Dawn

We walked the quiet streets before the sun came up.
In '67, soldiers marched here
Not knowing they were winning that war.

A cool breeze teases us, but there is fierce heat to come.
Already my lungs feel dry inside and my socks in dusty boots
Look dirty, though I washed them hard last night.

Through the Damascus Gate and into the Old City
Darkness comes down as if it's nightfall, rather than dawn.
The cobbles are wet from their morning bath.

We walk alone this early, stirring only the cats
Orange and white, gray and black, they are grubby
But clearly prospering, too.

Now up on the hill, just outside the Old City's walls
At the Mt. Zion gate, I ready for the day's work
Scraping through century after century of earth.

Off in the distance sits the Mount of Olives
And, just now, behind it, the glow of the sun rises
Bringing a new shine over this old, old city.

My Security

Like the hands of my mother
Holding me up as I learned to walk
These flashy painted metal sticks balance my steps

The feet are steely and indestructible
They hold fast to the earth and rock
And catch me when I stumble

The grips are soft and sure
The straps gripping each wrist
No matter the difficulty of the terrain

Trudging uphill or stumbling down
Rocky gravel, scree, or mud
They spring with my progress

Once I fell hard in a rock-strewn creek
Losing my grip the strap fell free
The pole tumbled into the rushing water

Bereft I shouted "oh shit"
And Henry heroically retrieved
My sense of security returned.

I Wish I Could Go On a Walk With Anne Lamott

We stroll along a flower-strewn path in California
Bees zooming about in that sunshine
Their buzzing zipping in and out of hearing
Birds are talking, too, because it is early morning
We have steaming cups of frothy coffee in our hands.

I watch her crazy-ass hair bounce along with her steps
She tells me how she survives thinking and writing about God
When everything other people say about that subject
Seems to make them so unrelentingly angry
Violent even.

She radiates calm and peacefulness, centering me
Though her words by themselves might feel jagged if you listen hard.
The sun rises higher and grows warmer
Toasting our faces and arms with the
Sound of her voice making sense out of God.

Damp Hands

She waited with others gathered in a ragged cluster
To jump into the stalls as the doors
Slammed behind each user
Some of whom did not
      Wash their hands

Or even snatch the briefest of glances
In the soap-spotted and water-splashed mirrors.
Strands of hair lingered
On the edges of sinks, primped
      By damp hands.

Who would go into a rest stop bathroom
And not wash their hands?
Back at the car, she glanced at the man's hands
On the steering wheel, hoping to see
      They were damp.

On I-77

I stare into the screen of my phone
To focus, to blot it all out
No! I can't look up to see
How close we are to the car in front of us
How near disaster, the trucks barreling by.

Don't ask me "did you see that?"
I'm trying to concentrate
On the email, the text, the news story,
You are distracting me from
My purposeful distraction.

If I look at the speedometer and see how fast
I'll not be able to stop the
Sharp intake of breath, the death grip
On the door's armrest and you'll be angry
And say "Do you want to drive?"

Which is not a valid question
You will not be a passenger
You will not slow down or
Let that guy into our lane
Or refrain from your narration.

What good will it do
If I get to say "I told you so"
If I say it from the crumpled heap
Of the car I am crushed in
Waiting for the jaws of life to extract me.

Stepping Sideways

The long weekend comes to an end
I am tired today without understanding why
Perhaps waiting for so many shoes to drop
Or the unfortunate shock surprise a death can bring.

Engineering change trying to manage
The unmanageable
Depending on the will and goodwill of others
Checking off lists that may or may not be complete.

Giving advice I can't take myself
Feeling just short of being sure
That it's OK to look forward to a big change
Stepping sideways instead of forward yet

Maybe it's just as easy to lay my head down
Out of the learned timing of it
To drive the tired away by
Subtracting awake expectations from the day.

Heart Attack
A Duplex

I lie awake at night worrying
It is futile and self-indulgent

It is futile and self-indulgent
And yet maybe I will find an answer

To how ignorance becomes virtuous
Why I can't find my way around hate

Though I know it's the only path out
And who cares who I hate anyway

I am only one small old white lady
Offering up my worrying in silence

Except that when I yell at the television
I feel like I'm having a heart attack

I feel like I'm having a heart attack
I lie awake at night worrying.

Who We're Going To Be

Watching my thoughts swirling
Sluicing around the white bowl
They haven't gone down the hole
Through the pipe
Run into the sewer
And down to the treatment plant.
Wet, soggy, the paper
Is coming apart but still it's holding up
My dreams, my hopes
What I think I know about you
What I think I know about myself.
And so the water keeps running
I jiggle the handle on the television
Tear off another page from the roll
Wadding it up, trying to be clean
To understand without obstruction
No clogs in my brain
It all needs to run free
The numbers flowing into my head
That will tell me who we're going to be.

Sunday Morning

Day begun with the first steps
Of the very young melting from
Sweetness that only lingers long enough
To contrast with grown up disappointment
Shrugging off the way the days can run
One into the other punctuated with
Bouts of holding back a feeling of weepiness
That isn't tears
Because those don't come when
There's no relief from them
No catharsis no sense once dry
The world will look different.

Holidays

Days like today remind us women
About things we've learned to do
Without direction, notice, or complaint
Work, determination
The will to always make it just so
No matter the obstacles.

We reject help
Finding it mostly annoying and of little
Actual assistance
Ever truer in the preparation of
A traditional family meal
We'd much rather simply do it ourselves.

And what of that irony?
We tirelessly undertake the tasks
And turn them into a great effort of dedication
Seasoned maybe here and there
With a pinch of self-pity
And a dash of being put-upon.

All the while rejecting any notion
Of volunteered assistance
Which we suspect isn't genuine anyway.
How do we learn such absurdities
So thoroughly?
All I know is, I'm not doing the dishes.

On The Way Home from the Doctor's Office

On the way home from the doctor's office
From *that* appointment
You know the one
The one many of us will eventually face
Unless we are fated to die in a blaze of destruction
Blown up or obliterated in dramatic fashion

Instead of just the mundane every day
"We can try X and see how you do"
Or "Some people have done well with X"
When you know, you *know* it's all bullshit
And you really have X number of hours or days
Or months to go

On the way home from *that* appointment
I will stop at the liquor store
And buy the most expensive bottle of single malt scotch they have
And then I'll stop and buy a carton of cigarettes
Non-menthol please
Something that has a decent hit of tar and nicotine.

The liquor will come in a fancy-ass box
I'll have to break a foil seal of gold and forest green
Then I'll open the top and extract the heavy bottle
With the hand that doesn't have a bandage stuck to it
Covering a wound into which some noxious concoction has been loaded
Or dark blood extracted, not that I watched.

Over the bottle's top I'll break another seal
Maybe scratching through some scarlet-colored wax
From the cupboard I'll fetch the heaviest short glass I have
And pour the heady amber liquid—the smell, oh the aroma
It is glorious and ashy and burned peaty wetness
No. No water, no ice to dilute the fragrance of the Highlands.

I'll envision myself sitting on a sharp outcrop in the gloaming light
Near the top of a Scottish Munro
Deciding to forgo the cigarette after all
Looking out over a valley
Where I'll see displayed before me a rainbow
And a golden eagle will fly across the view.

A Definition of Unity

In these times of division and derision and emboldenment
Of bluster and bombs and ignorance
Is there any way to make or become a whole
Here where I feel increasingly isolated and wonder about leaving

Is there a place to go
Or is the leaving everything
Where would I wake up and feel
The opposite of being divided

Does such a place exist
Or would the absence of diversity
The unvaried or uniform character of unity
Bring its own kind of isolation

It may be the exercise of being joined as a whole united
Is the only real purpose
And the inherent imperfections of the process
Their own beauty

Nowhere can I remember or imagine
Such a state of being in full agreement
Even with myself
In increasing isolation

Combining the parts so that they seem
To belong together is an imperfect exercise
The seeming is only that
The belonging is everything

Where do we find that feeling of concord
Is there a dot on a map
Where uniformity of character pervades
Where agreement of purpose envelops all

Feelings of oneness of mind are fleeting
In the best of circumstances
And don't reside in a geographic location
Your head does travel with you wherever you go

Maybe then it's better to fling ourselves
Full force at the very center of division
A place that exists everywhere after all
No matter how deep the cavern and dark the going

Perhaps harmony is actually found
In the questioning itself
The pushing and pulling the retreating and flinging
The paradox of individual expression and unity.

A version of this poem appeared in the anthology *Voices on Unity* as "A Question of Definitions: What Dictionaries Can Tell Us About Unity" published by Mountain State Press.

Little Birds

All of my old friends
The women, I mean
The ones I've not seen in years
Have changed into little birds.

Smaller, not just shorter
Shoulders rounded, backs hunched
Over chests that seem delicate
And fragile as little birds.

I am shocked when I see them
Their heads canted downward
Shuffling along, their hands clawed
Like the feet of little birds.

Only their voices have not altered
Their words still weighty
Their laughter ringing with vitality
No cheeping or thin songs of little birds.

When I return home I gaze
For a long time
In the mirror
Looking for little birds.

Sunday Night Is Yellow

Sunday night is yellow and cracked
It crinkles like unread ungraded papers
Tastes like the dust in my head
Smells like laundry left in the machine too long
So that now it must be washed again.

Sunday night is yellow and damp
A puddle of urine in the street
The smell hits your nose
You step over it carefully but it's as unavoidable
As Monday morning.

Sunday night is yellow and scratchy
Parching my brain
Impossible to quench
Burning through the dark
Rough and scaly.

Even though I am no longer
Sliding down to Mondays
It makes no difference
The yellow
Persists.

Elmwood Cemetery #1

We're walking in the dark each morning now
Altering our route at the onset to stay in patches of light
So that my propensity for falling will be abated.
By the time we get to the cemetery
The morning's brilliance rises behind the railroad trestle.
We search the old trees for signs of change
First will come the dogwoods with burgundy and crimson hues
And there, is that ancient maple showing tangerine glints?
The maintenance crew truck rumbles by with a nod
And we know that soon mowers will be replaced by blowers.

Elmwood Cemetery #2
A Pandemic Sonnet

Old trees, ancient and durable
Wave rickety and splintering in the breeze
Tall or wide their statements immutable
Even in the face of the coming freeze.

Branches and limbs lean and bend
Sometimes breaking with cracking violence
Leaving scattered remnants later to lend
The piles of curbside refuse a spikey countenance.

But floating above the noise of squeaking bark
Whirling and splashing around my shoes
The leaves lend grace in their dancing arcs
And decorate the sky with the season's hues.

The clanking and spitting of the mowers
Will soon be replaced with the oscillating thrum of blowers.

The House Inside My Head

I take it wherever I go
Everywhere I move, it is with me
From mountains, to cities
With rivers, and lakes, and bustle
Or quiet. It doesn't matter.

You know how people tell you that
You can't run away from your troubles?
Well hell's bells, I'm here to tell you
No matter what house you think you live in
You can't run away from shit.

Your house is where you are right now
Your home is inside your head
And sure, you can distract yourself for a while
Some people make a career out of distracting themselves

Make up a whole story about where they are
Who they are…
But we're all still, no kidding
Living at home
In the house inside our heads.

Chris Arvidson was born and grew up in Michigan. She has worked in national politics in Washington, D.C., and as a nonprofit communications and development professional at Habitat for Humanity, in higher education, and with two land conservancies. She holds a B.A. from Olivet College, an M.A. from UNC Charlotte, and an M.F.A. from Goucher College.

Chris has been an adjunct instructor at Robert Morris University and at UNC Charlotte. Currently she teaches creative writing at UNC Charlotte, and occasionally courses related to her lifelong passion for baseball. She has co-edited three anthologies in which her own work appears: *Mountain Memoirs: An Ashe County Anthology* (Main Street Rag), *Reflections on the New River: New Essays, Poems and Personal Stories* (McFarland), and *The Love of Baseball: Essays by Lifelong Fans* (McFarland). She has published an essay and poetry in *Nines: A Journal of Baseball History & Culture*.

www.ingramcontent.com/pod-product-compliance
Lightning Source LLC
LaVergne TN
LVHW041520070426
835507LV00012B/1712